Comrades in Arms

COMRADES IN ARMS

The Power of Pursuing Christ
in the
Company of Other Men

By
Rob Fischer

COMRADES IN ARMS
Copyright ©2013 Rob Fischer

Published by **Fischer Publishing**
14706 E. Queen Ave.
Spokane Valley, WA 99216

Scripture quotations taken from the HOLY BIBLE,
NEW INTERNATIONAL VERSION (NIV), Copyright © 1973,
1978, 1984 by International Bible Society. All Scripture
Quotations are taken from the NIV unless otherwise noted.

Scripture quotations marked (ESV) are from The Holy Bible,
English Standard Version®(ESV®), copyright © 2001 by Crossway,
a publishing ministry of Good News Publishers.
Used by permission. All rights reserved.

Scripture quotations marked (NLT) are taken from the Holy Bible,
New Living Translation, copyright © 1996.
Used by permission of Tyndale House Publishers, Inc.,
Wheaton, Illinois 60189. All rights reserved.

Scripture quotations marked MSG are taken from *The Message*.
Copyright © 1993, 1994, 1995, 1996, 2000, 2001, 2002.
Used by permission of NavPress Publishing Group

Acknowledgements

I am deeply grateful to the *comrades in arms* in my life. Teamed up with them we have watched God perform his transforming work in our lives. We have witnessed the power of God magnified through our partnerships in a way not possible for an individual trying to go it alone. My walk with Christ is deeper and my life is exceedingly richer as a result of their spiritual partnerships.

At the risk of overlooking someone, I dedicate this book to these men, my comrades in arms: Ed Cutler, Greg Grebe, Jay Pullins, Paul Biederman, Chris Keffalos, Ron Mancini, Dave Burris, Perry Underwood, Ray Edwards, and my brother Mark Fischer. Thank you, guys!

Table of Contents

Foreword 9
Introduction 13

Chapter One
SPIRITUAL PARTNERSHIP FOR SPIRITUAL TRANSFORMATION ... 21

Chapter Two
NEGLECTED PARTNERSHIPS 31

Chapter Three
CHARACTERISTICS OF SPIRITUAL PARTNERSHIP
(*Jesus' Pattern for Spiritual Partnership*) 41

Chapter Four
CHALLENGE EACH OTHER BOLDLY IN GOD'S WORD 55

Chapter Five
WHAT DOES SPIRITUAL PARTNERSHIP LOOK LIKE? 61

FAQs about Partnerships 73
Launch Your Spiritual Partnership 77

Foreword

Rob Fischer and I have been spiritual partners for the better part of six years. This partnership has been a catalyst for my spiritual growth, and has positively impacted every area of my life. Spiritual partnership has not always been *comfortable*, but it has always been *beneficial*, propelling me into deeper relationship with Christ.

The title of this little book is appropriate. When Christian men stand together on the battlefield of life, we are in fact "comrades in arms." In the company of other men who are committed to Christ, we accomplish much more than we ever could alone.

When I met Rob, I had only just recently come back to Christ after many years of rebelling against the Lord and my Christian upbringing. I was a "cautious Christian," with "commitment phobia." I was willing to come to church on most Sundays, but very skeptical of making any kind of commitment beyond that.

I enrolled in a course that Rob was facilitating, and was surprised to learn that one part of this course involved something called "spiritual partnership." Discussing the *idea* of spiritual partnership didn't bother me, but when I found out I was expected to actually *form* such a partnership, I felt panicky.

I wondered: *How much time will this take? What will I have to tell this person? Can I trust them to keep my secrets? Am I even willing to reveal any secrets?* Honestly, I didn't want any part of this "spiritual partnership" thing. But I did it anyway. Awkwardly. With sometimes messy results at first.

I would never go back.

Men tend to be drawn to the idea of the "rugged individualist." We like to think of ourselves as the "strong, silent type." Like Clint Eastwood in an old Western film, we long to be gun slingers who rely on our own skills to get through life.

God has something better in mind. He calls us to rely on him, and he also calls us to team up with other men.

Almost all of my spiritual growth has come when I was well outside my comfort zone. And I am most often forced outside that comfort zone through spiritual partnerships. These intentional relationships with other men have challenged me to grow, forced me to make decisions I would have otherwise avoided, and lifted me up during difficult times in my life.

Jesus said that his disciples would be known by their love for one another. Loving one another is not simply a poetic idea. Love for our brothers is not an abstract spiritual concept. *Love looks like something.* That something, I'm convinced, is what this book is about.

As you read the following pages, I urge you to ask yourself: "How is God speaking to me through what I'm reading?"

One of the questions I love to ask my spiritual partners, and hear them ask me, is "What is God doing in your life?"

I propose to you that one thing the Lord has done in your life is to put this book in your hands. I wonder how he will use it to draw you closer to him?

In his Service,
—Ray Edwards

Introduction

*Do all that is in your heart. Do as you wish.
Behold, I am with you heart and soul.*
— 1 Samuel 14:7 ESV —

When I was twelve years old I went to camp for the first time. One of the highlights of the camp experience for us was swimming in the lake on a hot summer day. But monitoring a couple hundred high-energy boys in the water was a daunting responsibility for the camp staff! There were too many boys and too few staff to provide a safe swimming environment.

To make swimming safe the camp staff established the "buddy-system." Each boy was assigned a buddy. We were not allowed in the water without our buddy. And when the whistle blew each boy grabbed the hand of his buddy and we raised our hands high to show that we had our buddy. In this way everyone was safe and accounted for.

Fast forward about seven years. As a young man I was hired by a Christian organization to evangelize the villages along the Oregon coast. I had rebuilt a 1958 VW van into a camper for this purpose that served as my mobile office and home. The prospect of serving God in this pioneer way appealed to my adventurous nature. That is until I actually embarked on this ministry. What I quickly discovered was that doing ministry solo is unnatural, ineffective, and very lonely. I desperately needed a buddy!

Ten years later, as a missionary in Austria, I remember agonizing over the absence of spiritual camaraderie in my life. I needed someone to come along side me in ministry—not a mentor, a coach, or even necessarily a co-worker, but a spiritual partner—a comrade in arms. I wanted someone to pray with; to encourage and be encouraged; someone to stand with me. I longed for someone with whom I could discuss and debate Scripture on a deep personal level. I craved a *comrade-in-arms* relationship with another man. I needed a confidant with whom I could share my struggles, not merely to empathize with me, but to challenge me boldly and permit me to challenge him boldly as well.

Years later, as a manager in a large company, again I felt a nagging void in my life for a man or men with whom I could team-up spiritually. I was also a husband, father of teens, an elder in our church, leading multiple ministries, but I had no *comrade in arms*. The irony of this period of my life was that I had Christian friends with whom I could be transparent. *We mistook transparency in our relationships for spiritual partnership*, but there were no courageous challenges and therefore no life change. Such openness without challenge for spiritual transformation emasculates the potential of what it means to be spiritual comrades in arms.

There are some great examples of this *comrade-in-arms relationship* between men in the Scriptures. In 1 Samuel 14, we read the valorous account of Jonathan and his armor-bearer. From this story we don't even learn the name of Jonathan's armor-bearer. What we do know about him is his character, his courage and his loyalty to Jonathan, even when Jonathan challenged the Philistines against insurmountable odds.

We pick up the account in 1 Samuel 14:6 ESV, "Jonathan said to the young man who carried his armor, 'Come, let us go over to the garrison of these uncircumcised. It may be that the Lord will work for us, for nothing can hinder the Lord from saving by many or by few.'" While Jonathan's faith in the Lord's sovereignty and power are evident here, we also know that Jonathan did not say to his armor-bearer, "You stay here while I go over and attack the Philistines." Jonathan needed his armor-bearer with him.

I love the armor-bearer's response to Jonathan, "Do all that is in your heart. Do as you wish. Behold, I am with you heart and soul." (1 Samuel 14:7 ESV) In the remaining verses of this chapter we learn how Jonathan and his armor-bearer fought valiantly and won a huge victory for Israel. In teaming up together, they also teamed up with God, who sent a panic into the ranks of the Philistines and routed them before Jonathan and his armor-bearer (1 Samuel 14:15 & 23).

Jonathan must have really bought into the value of a comrade-in-arms, because he also struck such a partnership with David. "Jonathan was deeply impressed with David—an immediate bond was forged between them. He became totally committed to David. From that point on he would be David's number-one advocate and friend." (1 Samuel 18:1 MSG)

Sometime later, Jonathan's own father Saul was hunting for David trying to kill him. As you can imagine, this was a very dark time in David's life. But we find a bright spot when Jonathan secretly visited him, "And Saul's son Jonathan went to David at Horesh and helped him find strength in God." (1 Samuel 23:16) That's what spiritual comrades in arms do—they help each other find strength in God.

In Acts 16, we read about Paul and Silas in Philippi. There they were publicly ridiculed, stripped, flogged, thrown into jail, and placed in the inner cell with their feet in the stocks. In the middle of their suffering and pain, Paul and Silas mustered the courage and strength to pray and sing hymns together. I cannot make the claim that either of these two brave Christ-followers would not have prayed or sung hymns *without* the company and encouragement of the other. But the fact remains that *together* they prayed and sang in the face of severe persecution. And God used their team effort to lead the jailer and his family to Christ.

Most of us are not warriors in the sense of David or Jonathan and his armor-bearer. And few of us have ever been beaten and imprisoned for our faith like Paul and Silas. Yet, *we are in a battle:*

> *Finally, be strong in the Lord and in the strength of his might. Put on the whole armor of God, that you may be able to stand against the schemes of the devil. For we do not wrestle against flesh and blood, but against the rulers, against the authorities, against the cosmic powers over this present darkness, against the spiritual forces of evil in the heavenly places. Therefore take up the whole armor of God, that you may be able to withstand in the evil day, and having done all, to stand firm.*
> *– Ephesians 6:10-13 ESV*

But this book is not about the important topic of spiritual armor. This book is about something else so basic that we easily overlook it and go into battle totally unprepared and vulnerable. This oft-missed foundational element in this passage about our spiritual warfare is *our comrades in arms*. How do I glean that from this passage in Ephesians?

First, all of the pronouns in Paul's commands in Ephesians 6:10-20 are *plural*. Paul is not writing to individual soldiers, but to the squad, platoon, or battalion. We are not in this battle alone and we are fools to think we can fight it alone, or were ever meant to fight it alone.

A second reason this passage in Ephesians focuses on our comrades in arms appears in verses 17-19. Although the meaning is clear in any of the common versions, here is Eugene Petersen's paraphrase from the Message:

> *God's Word is an indispensable weapon. In the same way, prayer is essential in this ongoing warfare. Pray hard and long. Pray for your brothers and sisters. Keep your eyes open. Keep each other's spirits up so that no one falls behind or drops out. And don't forget to pray for me.*
> *– Ephesians 6:17-19 MSG*

Paul's urgent reminder of the powerful weapon of prayer draws attention to our interaction with the Holy Spirit and with each other in the fray. This reminds us of the way Jonathan helped David find strength in the Lord. The battles we fight for Christ's character to be formed in us, for our purity, for our bold and holy witness in a lost world, for our integrity as husbands, fathers, and employees or employers; all of these battles cannot and should not be attempted alone!

God has ordained that we should each team up with other men around us. In warfare, the one who goes off by himself and leaves his unit is AWOL. He's a deserter. The victors team up together. They fight together. They care for and support one another. This book is a practical book on how to do that in everyday life.

Who are you standing with? Who is standing with you? Who's your buddy? Who is your comrade in arms? Who is your spiritual partner? Following Christ is not a solo endeavor. If you have longed for deep spiritual partnership like I have, or simply desire to grow in Christ and help others grow in their relationship with Christ, then read on.

"Jonathan became one in spirit with David, and he loved him as himself." – 1 Samuel 18:1

Before we go on I'd like to settle one small issue. I have wracked my brain and tapped into the minds of others for over ten years to come up with a suitable, culturally relevant, manly term for *spiritual partnerships*. The title of this book, **COMRADES IN ARMS**, is a cool term meaning *fellow soldiers*. *Comrades in arms* may be more masculine, but is not as versatile as the term *spiritual partnership*. I'm convinced that what we call it is not so important as long as we're engaged in it! As a man to men, don't let a term derail you!

—*Rob Fischer*

Discussion Questions

1. What particular point in this chapter impacted you most?

2. Think of a time when you've wished you had a comrade in arms to stand with you and help you find strength in God. What was that situation? In what ways would a comrade in arms have helped you?

3. Discuss the statement: "God has ordained that we should each team up with other men around us. In warfare, the one who goes off by himself and leaves his unit is AWOL. He's a deserter. The victors team up together. They fight together. They care for and support one another."

4. To what extent do you think having a comrade in arms—a spiritual partner—would help you walk more resolutely and consistently with Jesus Christ?

5. On a scale of 1-10, 10 being high, how ready and willing are you to move forward toward partnership with a comrade in arms?

Chapter One
SPIRITUAL PARTNERSHIP
FOR SPIRITUAL TRANSFORMATION

*Two are better than one,
because they have a good return for their labor*
— Ecclesiastes 4:9 —

Spiritual partnerships with other followers are one of the most powerful, yet most neglected means for life change in Christ we have available to us! Partnering with others is a *transformational relationship* in which we focus on mutually spurring one another on to growth in Christ (Hebrews 10:24). *Spiritual transformation takes place in spiritual partnerships.* This holds true for at least five reasons.

First, we become like those with whom we spend time whether we plan for it or not. Some years ago, a friend of mine, Greg, was coaching me in the skills of winter alpine hiking in the Chugach Range of Alaska. Greg was in front of me kick-stepping and setting trail up a very steep, snow-covered grade. Since it is much easier to follow in the exact footsteps of the person breaking trail, I stepped in Greg's tracks mimicking his exact foot placement and stride.

Greg, however, has an unusual quirk resulting from reconstructive surgery on his left foot. His left foot is splayed outward at a significant angle. On our climb, I had been following Greg's footsteps for perhaps 45 minutes when I looked down and started to laugh out loud. Without knowing it, by following Greg's footsteps I was turning my left foot out and walking just like him!

We become like those we spend time with—for good or for bad. Proverbs 27:17 explains, "As iron sharpens iron, so one person sharpens another." Spiritual partners help sharpen and hone each other. In 1 Corinthians 11:1, Paul urges the Corinthian followers of Christ, "Follow my example, as I follow the example of Christ." Later in that letter Paul also warns, "Do not be misled: 'Bad company corrupts good character.'" (1 Corinthians 15:33) *We become like those with whom we spend time.*

Second, spiritual partnerships are a biblical model for life change. This is another way of saying that *spiritual partnerships are a biblical model for discipleship*. Discipleship describes the process of following Jesus and growing in an ever-deepening relationship with him. The result of our ever-deepening relationship with Christ is a transformed life. As we follow Jesus he changes us and we become more like him in our character, motivations, thoughts, words and actions.

We sometimes erroneously think of discipleship in terms of a program or class that a new believer attends. But discipleship is a *lifelong process* that every follower of Jesus Christ engages in continually. Even as an old man, Paul explained that he still longed to know Christ better. Paul admitted that he had not yet "arrived," but continued to "press on to take hold of that for which Christ Jesus took hold of him" (Philippians 3:12). As followers of Jesus Christ, we all need to be on a trajectory of life change in Jesus Christ. One of the best ways to stay engaged in our personal discipleship process is through spiritual partnership.

Spiritual partnerships were Jesus' pattern with his disciples and the apostles' pattern for ministry. The Scriptures explain that Jesus chose his twelve disciples, "that he might spend time with them and that he might train them for kingdom work." (Mark 3:14 paraphrase) Jesus' example reveals at least five elements of spiritual partnership that we'll look at later.

Notice the pattern of spiritual partnership that is stamped all over Paul's description of his relationship with Philemon.

> *I always thank my God as I remember you in my prayers, because I hear about your love for all his holy people and your faith in the Lord Jesus. I pray that your partnership with us in the faith may be effective in deepening your understanding of every good thing we share for the sake of Christ. Your love has given me great joy and en-*

> *couragement, because you, brother, have refreshed the hearts of the Lord's people. (Philemon 1:4-7)*

On the foundation of their spiritual partnership, Paul courageously challenged Philemon to receive back his runaway slave Onesimus as a brother in Christ (Philemon 1:10-21).

Our relationship with the Holy Spirit is another clear example in which we see the biblical pattern of spiritual partnerships. In John 14:16-17 ESV, Jesus explained:

> *I will ask the Father, and he will give you another Helper, to be with you forever, even the Spirit of truth, whom the world cannot receive, because it neither sees him nor knows him. You know him, for he dwells with you and will be in you.*

That word "Helper" indicates "someone called alongside." Some translations render "Helper" as our Advocate or Intercessor.

The Holy Spirit is our ultimate spiritual partner. He teaches us about Christ and draws us closer in our relationship with him and with others. In the examples of spiritual partnership that I give from my own life, you'll notice a pattern. Namely, my spiritual partnerships frequently occur in the context of walking, hiking or snowshoeing. Your spiritual partnerships may not be as outdoor-oriented as mine, but consider what Paul tells us about our spiritual partnership with the Holy Spirit in Galatians 5:16-26. In this passage, Paul urges us to: *"walk* by the Spirit;" "be *led* by the Spirit;" *"live* by the Spirit;" and *"keep in step* with the Spirit." Paul's expressions provide us with a graphic image of what our spiritual partnership should look like with the Spirit of Christ who dwells within us.

Third, spiritual partnerships offer a strategic approach to life change in Jesus Christ because the whole is greater than the sum of its parts. Ecclesiastes 4:9 NLT, explains, "Two people can accomplish more than twice as much as one; they get a better return for their labor."

A couple I know raises draft horses. This couple explained to me that one draft horse can pull 3,000 pounds dead weight. But two draft horses teamed together can pull 8,000 pounds dead weight! A similar phenomenon occurs in our spiritual partnerships with other followers of Christ. "Yoked together" with them, Christ does a great deal more in and through us than when we try to go it alone.

In the past eleven years, God has changed me more through the men I'm spiritually partnered with than by any other means. Just like with the draft horses, spiritual partnerships enable us to harness God's grace in our lives so we can pull each other forward in our pursuit of Christ. "As iron sharpens iron, so one person sharpens another." (Proverbs 27:17)

There are some sins, thought patterns or addictions that we may never be able to overcome without the spiritual partnership of another. A friend of mine works with men to help them overcome sexual addiction. After years of experience, he concludes that spiritual partnerships are essential to breaking such addictions. Additionally, we all have blind spots in our lives that we need others to point out to us. Without spiritual partnership we may go blundering through life, not realizing the negative impact we're having on others.

Fourth, spiritual partnerships provide needed protection. Ecclesiastes 4:12 NLT, tells us, "A person standing alone can be attacked and defeated, but two can stand back-to-back and conquer." We need each other to "watch each other's backs." God never intended for us to stand alone. Often, we need protection from ourselves and the dumb things we say and do. A spiritual partner can point out in our lives what we overlook.

Have you ever watched lions single out and isolate a gazelle or zebra from its herd and take it down for the kill? Peter tells us, "Your enemy the devil prowls around like a roaring lion looking for someone to devour." (1 Peter 5:8) One of the evil one's deadly tricks is to isolate us from other followers of Christ and take us down. If you've known Christ for any length of time, you've probably experienced what I'm talking about. Ironically, when we're feeling down, beat up and unloved, we typically crawl off by ourselves like an injured animal and Satan attacks! Resist the tendency to isolate and ask a brother to stand with you.

Many men struggle with spiritual partnership. Somewhere along the line we've bought into the lie that we have to do everything solo, or we jeopardize our manhood! This notion is based in pride and stupidity. I know, because I'm a man. I've made some really foolish mistakes trying to go it alone. Spiritual partnership is not a sign of weakness, but of strength and wisdom. David slew a bear and lion with his bare hands, and a giant with a sling. Yet he deeply valued his spiritual partnership with Jonathan and took strength from it. David's spiritual partnership with Jonathan didn't render him less of a man. On the contrary, Jonathan undoubtedly gained from this partnership as well.

When I lived and hiked in Alaska, I adhered to one of the cardinal rules of back country trekking in Alaska. That cardinal rule is: *never go into the wilderness alone.* The same applies in all of life. We need the spiritual protection and camaraderie that spiritual partnerships provide.

Fifth, the nature of the change God wants to bring about in us is chiefly relational. In fact, Christlikeness can be described as exhibiting Christ's relational characteristics. Think about it, we cannot grow in love without practicing love *with others*. We exercise forgiveness, forbearance, kindness, gentleness, hospitality, showing honor, living in harmony, speaking truthfully, sharing with those in need, walking in purity, and wholesome talk all *in the context of relationships*. Apart from *relationships* those character traits have no context for expression and cannot be fully developed.

How can we learn to love without being thrust into relationships in which love is required? And what better way to learn to love than by watching other followers of Christ model love and coach us in it!

During basic training in the Army, I enjoyed participating in what they called the *confidence course*. The confidence course was a challenge or ropes course "on steroids!" One particular element especially intrigued me. It was a three-story structure built on four vertical telephone poles, their ends anchored in the ground. As these four vertical poles rose from the ground, they angled out away from each other. The result was that their tops were much farther from each other than their bases were at ground level. Each successive platform was about nine feet above the lower one. And because the poles angled outward, each platform above extended farther out than the one below it.

The design of this element made it virtually impossible for an *individual* to master it alone. A person simply could not climb it solo. But with a partner *both* could assist each other and climb to the top, and that's what we did. A life of following Christ and growing in him is like that confidence course element. The nature of the change God wants to bring about in us *requires* camaraderie or partnership with other followers of Christ.

Perhaps some who are reading this think that I'm exaggerating making that previous statement. You may think that growing in Christ might be *easier* with the help of others, but not *necessary*. I can assure you, I am not exaggerating! We *cannot* go it alone. We need each other, because the changes God wants to bring about in us *require interaction with each other* to bring them about. It is simply *not possible* to grow in love or any of the other relational character traits of Christ apart from relationships with others.

Paul speaks of the correlation between our spiritual growth and our relationship with other followers of Christ in Ephesians 4. In verses 15-16 he explains:

> *Instead, speaking the truth in love, we will grow to become in every respect the mature body of him who is the head, that is, Christ. From him the whole body, joined and held together by every supporting ligament, grows and builds itself up in love, as each part does its work.*

The nature of the change that God seeks to bring about in us is chiefly relational and therefore must take place in the context of relationships. Spiritual partnerships with other followers of Christ provide a fertile environment for our growth to flourish.

Life change takes place in spiritual partnerships, because...

- We become like those with whom we spend time
- Spiritual partnerships are a biblical model for life change
- The whole is greater than the sum of its parts
- Spiritual partnerships provide needed protection
- The nature of the change God wants to bring about in us is chiefly relational

Discussion Questions

1. What particular point in this chapter impacted you most?

2. Think of someone with whom you've spent some significant time. In what ways have you taken on some of the characteristics or behavior of this person? Why is it that others can influence us so profoundly—for good or for bad?

3. How does Rob define *discipleship?* Where are you on your lifelong journey with Jesus?

4. Think of another example that demonstrates the principle that "two can accomplish more than twice as much as one."

5. In what specific areas of your life do you most need a comrade in arms to "watch your back"?

6. Why are we as men so prone to try to go it alone? Why is it so vital that partner spiritually with other men?

Chapter Two
NEGLECTED PARTNERSHIPS

A person standing alone can be attacked and defeated,
but two can stand back-to-back and conquer.
— Ecclesiastes 4:12 NLT —

I mentioned earlier that spiritual partnerships are one of the most powerful, yet most *neglected* means that Christ uses to change us. We've seen briefly why spiritual partnerships are so essential, but why do we neglect such partnerships? Why do so many of us go AWOL?

A number of years ago, I watched a pastor struggle through the most gut-wrenching experience of his life. This man had pastored a country church for many years in a tiny town with a vision for what God could do in a community that was ever dwindling. God used this pastor and his church powerfully and extensively in that community and beyond.

But this pastor lacked a spiritual partner and rejected the offer of one. He had no one to speak into his life. He had no one to ask him tough questions and challenge him. He had no one in whom he could or would confide. Finally, as a result of his preoccupation with one particular teaching in Scripture to the exclusion of others, he began to alienate people in the church. There were hurt feelings, misunderstandings, and cruel accusations.

Soon his church asked him to leave under unpleasant circumstances. Without a spiritual partner to "sharpen" him, he did not take their criticism well and regressed into a state of self-pity, feeling persecuted and falsely accused. By the time he finally left the church, there was a lot of damage, confusion and anger on both sides. If this man had had a spiritual partner through all of this, I believe this situation could have ended well.

We neglect spiritual partnerships for a number of reasons. First, like that pastor, *many of us pretend we are loners*. To put it plainly, we are proud. We don't see our need for others. We think we should be able to say we did it ourselves—without the help of others. We somehow see ourselves as above others or better than others, so we strike off on our own. This loner mentality is not a scriptural approach to work, ministry, or life and leads to trouble and often utter failure.

When I was a child attending elementary school, my teachers often gave an individual assignment to the students in the classroom. With the assignment, a spirit of competition arose in the classroom to see who could complete their work before anyone else. The early finishers would put their pencils down noisily, cross their arms, and look around smugly as if to say, "Look at me, I'm finished! Why aren't you?"

I believe the attitude of many Christians is like those grade-schoolers. We think that if we have *our* lives in order, *our* responsibility ends there. And we look around smugly at others wondering why they are not where we are spiritually. But as we saw earlier from Ephesians 4:15-16, spiritual growth is a *team sport*. We cannot afford to be satisfied with our own spiritual growth if those around us are floundering. In fact, if we think we're spiritual (Christlike), but attempt to practice our spirituality lacking deep relationships with others, we have both deluded ourselves and we're cheating others. We've gone AWOL.

No sooner did Jesus embark on his ministry, than he chose twelve, "that they might be with him" (Mark 3:14). When he sent them out to preach, he sent them out in *pairs*. And after Jesus ascended into heaven, his apostles and other followers banded together and stuck together. It's almost impossible to find a time when Paul was not working alongside other co-workers. Spiritual partnership was the *norm* in the early church.

Let's look at spiritual partnership from others' viewpoint instead of ours for a moment. What if someone were to approach us and sincerely request that we step into a spiritual partnership with them? Looking at spiritual partnership from the vantage point of the other person gives us a different perspective. Even if we don't recognize our own need for spiritual partnership, are we willing to meet another's need for it? Are we willing to stand as a comrade in arms with another man to help him succeed in his marriage, career, as a father, and follower of Christ?

Spiritual partnership is not solely about us. When we enter into a spiritual partnership with someone, we are actively prodding and encouraging each other toward Jesus Christ and life change. Spiritual partnership is a true privilege in which we play the role of a change agent in someone else's life. God will use us to spur and propel them into deeper relationship with him resulting in a transformed life. Never underestimate the potential of Christ's impact through you in another man's life.

Second, we also neglect spiritual partnership *because we don't know how to practice it*. For many years I had longed for spiritual partnership but didn't know what to call it or how to cultivate it. When we moved to Alaska, the church we worked with promoted spiritual partnerships as a core value. So I was not surprised when Ed approached me one day and asked if I would consider stepping into spiritual partnership with him. I told him I would, but that I really wasn't sure what spiritual partnership looked like. He laughed and admitted that he didn't know either, so we decided to simply begin meeting weekly to hike and pray and figure it out.

Over the next five years, Ed and I met weekly to pray with each other as we hiked or snow-shoed through the foothills of the Chugach Mountains. We shared our struggles, temptations and victories with each other and prayed for each other's growth in Christ. We boldly challenged each other from God's Word. Our relationship grew rich and life-changing. God has used my spiritual partnership with

Ed and other men over the past eleven years to change my life profoundly. I wouldn't be without a spiritual partner—a comrade in arms today. In fact, when we left Alaska and moved back to Spokane, one of the first things I did was contact a friend here and establish a spiritual partnership with him.

Another element in not knowing how to practice spiritual partnership has to do with discipleship. Many of us view discipleship as hierarchical. We tend to see discipleship as something more mature Christians do for newer, younger followers of Christ. This downward view of discipleship can be very misleading. As we've already discussed, all followers of Christ are engaged in the lifelong process of discipleship. In this respect, we're all on a level playing field. We all need discipling.

With a purely hierarchical view of discipleship, someone might approach you and say, "I'd like to disciple you." How would that make you feel? It feels top-down to me. One is the *teacher* and the other the *learner*. Would you wonder about this person's motives? Do they think they've arrived? Do they think I'm that pathetic?! Would their approach make me feel *guilty* if I turned them down? Many would run scared from such an invitation.

If on the other hand, someone comes up to you and says, "I've been praying for a comrade in arms, for someone to partner with me spiritually. Would you consider being my spiritual partner/my comrade in arms?" There's humility there. Most of us would feel honored to be asked. Spiritual partnership is *mutual* and *reciprocal*. We may have to decline this request for other reasons, but it won't be because we're turned off by this guy's approach.

A third reason we neglect spiritual partnership has to do with the fact that *spiritual partnership is a discipline and a skill. We must be deliberate and work hard to cultivate spiritual partnership.* Like a garden overgrown with weeds, or tools gone rusty without care, so too any relationship will soon deteriorate with neglect. Many of us maintain *acquaintances* hoping to meet our need for true spiritual partnership. But we can drown in a sea of acquaintances while thirsting for genuine partnership.

Ed and I discovered the hard work of spiritual partnerships and we gave ourselves to it. Spiritual partnership involves authentic living before each other. We model for each other what it means to follow Christ. We imitate Christ and his character openly in our spiritual partnership. We deliberately spur each other on to deeper relationship in Christ.

In fact, *boldly challenging each other in real life issues is the catalyst for life change in Christ.* This bold challenge is what sets spiritual partnership apart from other relationships. The freedom we grant each other in a spiritual partnership to courageously challenge each other is what distinguishes these relationships as *transformational*.

A fourth reason that may keep us from entering into a spiritual partnership is *fear*. Fear may simply be embarrassment, shyness, or could stem from past wounds in previous relationships. If fear is coming from simply being shy or social discomfort—be courageous and get over it! As someone has said, "Courage is not the absence of fear. Courage acknowledges the fear and acts in spite of it." The stakes are too high to continue neglecting spiritual partnership. It's often fear that drives a man to go AWOL.

If on the other hand, fear is the product of past broken relationships and hurts, then pray and ask God for a spiritual partner who will be able to help you in this area. Look for a spiritual partner who genuinely wants to know Christ better and become like Christ.

The characteristics of spiritual partnership do much to dispel these reasons for neglecting spiritual partnership. Let's move on to the next chapter to look at the characteristics of spiritual partnerships.

Discussion Questions

1. What particular point in this chapter impacted you most?

2. Why do so many men neglect spiritual partnerships and go AWOL?

3. If we are neglecting spiritual partnership with other men, how might we be cheating *them?* Why is spiritual partnership not solely about us?

4. Rob confesses that when he was asked to step into spiritual partnership with Ed, Rob didn't know exactly what that meant or what it would look like. At this point in time, how would you rate your level of understanding with spiritual partnership? (Self-rate 1-10, with 10 being high.)

5. Explain the difference between an acquaintance or even a friend and a spiritual partner. Why is it that spiritual partnership promotes deeper relationship with Christ?

6. Of the four reasons Rob lists that may prevent us from entering into a spiritual partnership, which one do you most closely identify with and why?

   1) we pretend we are loners;
   2) we don't know how to practice spiritual partnership;
   3) spiritual partnership is a discipline and skill and therefore hard work; and,
   4) fear.

Chapter Three
CHARACTERISTICS OF SPIRITUAL PARTNERSHIP
(Jesus' Pattern for Spiritual Partnership)

*Jonathan became one in spirit with David,
and he loved him as himself.*
– 1 Samuel 18:1 –

From the Gospel records, we observe that Jesus stepped into spiritual partnership with his disciples. Because he is the Lord, his relationship with his disciples was not mutual and reciprocal like ours will be. But Jesus shows us the way when it comes to spiritual partnership. Jesus' example reveals at least five characteristics of spiritual partnership. First, Jesus demonstrated the pattern for spiritual partnership as *men with men and women with women* pursuing relationship with him.

This first characteristic of spiritual partnership is especially crucial for us. Men need to partner spiritually with other men and women with women. This gender-specific approach is vital first because it's most effective. Men know how men think and women know how women think. Each gender understands the struggles and temptations unique to that gender. Paul applies this strategy in his instructions to Titus in the second chapter of his letter to him (Titus 2:1-8).

Of course, if you are married, your spouse should be one of your spiritual partners. So our spouse is the exception to this gender-specific principle. We should share our joys and struggles with our spouse, pray with each other, and read the Word together. But in addition to our spouse, men need other men and women need other women to partner with spiritually.

Another reason that gender-specific spiritual partnership is so vital is for the sake of *propriety*. Spiritual partnership demands transparency. For instance, if a man and a woman who are not married begin to share intimate thoughts and struggles with each other, they are asking for trouble! They're placing themselves in a very vulnerable position in which sexual temptation is bound to present itself. Don't make the mistake of thinking you're above such temptation! Don't partner spiritually with a person of the opposite sex.

Especially in our culture today, which has deliberately sought to eliminate differences between men and women, some might think this gender-specific principle is archaic and prudish. So please allow me the following analogy. I am a woodworker. One of the tools I often use in my shop is a table saw. Because the table saw is a potentially dangerous tool, I always use a push-stick instead of my hand in order to slide stock through the saw.

Using a push-stick is the safe approach to operating a table saw. Would anyone accuse me of being old-fashioned or paranoid for using a push-stick? I don't think so. As a cautionary measure, we also deliberately cultivate gender-specific spiritual partnerships.

Furthermore, there's the issue of appearances. As followers of Christ, we strive to be blameless before others. But if a man and woman are spending significant time together alone under the guise of spiritual partnership, they may give others the impression that there's more going on there. Why give the evil one opportunity to tempt you and soil your witness for Christ before others? *Spiritual partners are men with men and women with women pursuing relationship with Jesus Christ.*

A second characteristic of spiritual partnership modeled by Christ is that *he spent time together with them in real life*. If you skim through the four Gospels, you'll notice that Jesus spent a lot of time with his disciples in real life situations. They went to weddings, funerals, dinners, the temple and the synagogue together. Jesus spent a lot of time with his disciples in a boat, walking, traveling from village to village, in homes and on hillsides and in market places.

Additionally, Jesus was unafraid to let his disciples see him tired, hungry, thirsty, angry, sad, grieved, mocked, and rejected. They experienced Jesus' response to the best and worst of times. He lived his life very publicly and openly before them.

Spending time together in real life is a hallmark of spiritual partnership. Think about it—if my spiritual partner only sees me at a coffee house or at church, he won't see how I interact with my wife and kids. He won't know how I handle myself in traffic, or at work, or at play. Spiritual partners need to spend time with each other in real life situations of all kinds. Many of the most striking spiritual moments of growth for Jesus' disciples occurred in everyday settings: fishing, in a boat, in a grain field, at a wedding, or on a hillside.

In recent years, I've been stretched and have grown as I've spent time with my spiritual partners in real life situations. I've watched their patience and tact when confronted with an angry driver or client. I've learned from them as they've exhibited tenderness toward their wives and children. I've been deeply moved by their kind words of encouragement offered to a cashier or waitress who was having a bad day. I've been convicted by their love and fervor for the Lord and challenged by their unmoving faith in our great God! As spiritual partners, *we need to spend time with each other in real life.*

A third characteristic of spiritual partnership is that *spiritual partners love and care for each other.* Jesus told his disciples, "Love one another. As I have loved you, so you must love one another." (John 13:34) Love and care for each other is the currency of spiritual partnership in Christ. Right before Jesus gave his disciples this command he demonstrated the full extent of his love for them by washing their feet. Following this loving, humble act, he said, "I have set you an example that you should do as I have done for you." (John 13:15)

Several years ago, I was leading a men's small group in which we had all agreed to partner spiritually. For two weeks in a row I noticed that Ted (not his real name) was not there. The Holy Spirit prompted me to call Ted. When he answered his phone, I could tell something was wrong, so I asked him to come clean with me. Ted explained that his business partner had swindled him out of his half of their business and in the process Ted had lost his car and his income. For two weeks, he'd been living on a credit card.

I immediately prayed with Ted over the phone and then asked permission to share his need with the other men in our group. These men rallied around their brother. Within a week, one man loaned Ted a car indefinitely; the group gave him a sizeable amount of cash to meet his immediate needs; and another man offered Ted a job. Ted was overwhelmed with the love and care he received from his spiritual partners!

Another less obvious expression of our love and care for each other as spiritual partners is the fact that we won't always partner spiritually with others just like us. One of my spiritual partners is a man who is very different from me in a number of ways: ethnically, background, family, career, and interests. God, however, brought us together and we've shared a unique spiritual bond now for many years. Be open to partnering spiritually with someone who is not necessarily just like you. What matters is that you both genuinely want to pursue Christ.

Also, the fact that spiritual partnerships are mutual and reciprocal does not require that the two spiritual partners be equally mature in Christ. Some of the greatest lessons I've learned in love and humility have been through relatively new or immature believers. The key in a spiritual partnership is that both partners long to know Christ better and team together to propel each other into deeper relationship with him.

As you meet with your spiritual partner, one of the best ways to express love and care for them is to listen actively and intently. Be there for them. *Spiritual partners love and care for each other.*

Fourth, *spiritual partners challenge each other boldly from God's Word*. For followers of Christ to be transparent and vulnerable with each other is fairly common and needs to be a core practice among spiritual partners. However, we have probably all experienced relationships in which we shared such transparency, yet we were frustrated that no life change seemed to result from our being vulnerable with each other.

Transparency or vulnerability with others is important, but by itself does not necessarily lead to life change in Christ. We must move on from vulnerability to what we call *transformational relationship.* (See accompanying diagram. Adapted from John Powell's, *Why Am I Afraid to Tell You Who I Am?*) In a transformational relationship, we give each other permission to speak into one another's lives, or challenge each other boldly from God's Word. In a transformational relationship, we intentionally propel each other into deeper relationship with Christ.

Characteristics of Spiritual Partnership | 47

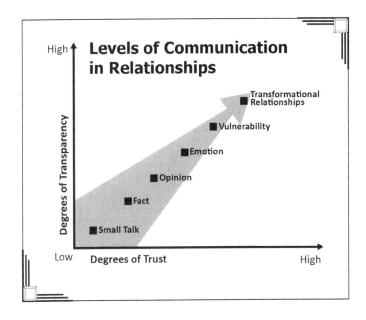

Transformational relationship is what sets spiritual partnership apart from other good relationships with followers of Christ. We fellowship with and may be vulnerable with other followers of Christ. But we will not likely enjoy transformational relationship with everyone. We all need spiritual partnerships in which we experience a high degree of transparency and trust, boldly challenging each other.

When I first begin meeting with a spiritual partner, we verbally grant each other permission to ask *tough questions* and to boldly challenge each other in following Christ. We ask each other questions like:

"What is God doing in your life right now?"

"What is God showing you from his Word?"

"What one thing in your life is preventing you from enjoying God fully?"

"In what ways are you currently leading your wife and family closer to the Lord?"

"How well are you loving your wife right now?"

"What are your greatest joys/challenges in walking with Jesus right now?"

"What's one thing you'd like to see Christ change in you?"

"In what ways is God using you to model Christ-likeness to others?"

Questions like these help move us into transformational relationship. When we pose questions like these, we want to listen humbly and intently, speak into each other's lives from God's Word and pray for each other. And if we catch each other thinking, speaking, or behaving in a way contrary to Christ, we tactfully yet boldly challenge each other from the Word.

Hebrews 10:24 provides the basis for this principle, "And let us consider how we may spur one another on toward love and good deeds." In other words, "Let's see how creative we can be in prodding each other toward Christlikeness!" Paul calls this, "Speaking the truth in love." (Ephesians 4:15) *Spiritual partners challenge each other boldly from God's Word.* This is such a crucial characteristic that I've devoted the next chapter solely to it.

Fifth, *spiritual partners pray for each other*. Jesus apparently prayed often and openly for his disciples. We know

Characteristics of Spiritual Partnership | 49

this because they heard his prayers and recorded some of them for our benefit as well. The Bible also encourages us that Jesus continues to pray for us today (Hebrews 7:25).

Paul urges us to "Pray in the Spirit on all occasions with all kinds of prayers and requests. With this in mind, be alert and always keep on praying for all the saints." (Ephesians 6:18) And James urges us to, "Confess your sins to each other and pray for each other." (James 5:16) Praying for each other as spiritual partners is one of the most loving, caring and powerful things we can do together! By praying for each other we come to the Lord on behalf of each other; we agree and team-up to present our requests to God; and we demonstrate before each other our love for God and for each other.

I believe that one of the keys to praying with each other effectively is to pray *conversationally*. Somewhere along the line, we've developed some very non-relational, non-conversational approaches to praying with God and others. These non-relational approaches produce distaste, avoidance and even fear of praying with others. By contrast, healthy, relational, conversational prayer with others follows these characteristics:

- ▶ Pray short, phrase or sentence prayers.
- ▶ Stay on a theme until it seems right to move on. Piggyback on each other's prayers.
- ▶ Keep your prayers vertical (don't use prayer to *preach* at others).

- Embrace silence as an opportunity to listen to God, transition, or process what's been prayed. Listen to the Holy Spirit and each other.

- Believe the best of each other.

These conversational guidelines are healthy and relational because they abide by principles that people commonly accept and expect in considerate conversations with others. I recommend following these guidelines anytime we're praying with others. Typically, we do not view longwinded monologues as considerate behavior in the context of healthy conversation. Nobody likes a "conversation hog"! Why then would we think that such behavior is alright in conversational prayer? Shouldn't conversational prayer represent the *best* in good relational characteristics?

Consider another example. In a well-functioning conversation, a polite person does not change the subject as long as that subject is still the focus of the conversation. Yet in much traditional group prayer, one person will pray about numerous subjects without ever coming up for air. Then those who follow fill their prayers again with a variety of disjointed, non-related topics. This behavior is crazy! Could it be that such anti-social behavior in public prayer is one reason so many Christians struggle when it comes to praying out loud with others?

As we nurture a rich culture of prayer with each other and the Lord, our hearts are united and we grow together in the grace of Jesus Christ.

Five Key Characteristics of Spiritual Partnerships

Life change takes place in spiritual partnerships.

- Men with men and women with women pursuing relationship with Christ
- Spend time together in real life
- Love and care for each other
- Challenge each other boldly from God's Word
- Pray with and for each other

In the next chapter, we'll take a closer look at what it means to challenge each other boldly from God's Word.

Discussion Questions

1. What particular point in this chapter impacted you most?

2. Why is it so vital that spiritual partnerships be gender-specific?

3. Mark 4:35-41 offers a great example of Jesus spending time with his disciples in real life. Read this account and explain how this real life experience became so impactful for Jesus' disciples. Why is it so important that spiritual partners spend time together in real life?

4. What are some ways we can express love and care for each other in the context of spiritual partnerships?

5. If you are meeting with a spiritual partner or small group as you work through this book, ask each other a couple of the *tough questions* listed in this chapter. What impact do questions like these have on you?

6. Again, if you are working through this book with others, take time to pray for each other. Try practicing the skills of conversational prayer listed in this chapter as you pray.

Chapter Four
CHALLENGE EACH OTHER BOLDLY IN GOD'S WORD

Jonathan went to David at Horesh and
helped him find strength in God.
— 1 Samuel 23:16 —

In the previous chapter, we saw that challenging each other boldly in God's Word is a key characteristic of spiritual partnerships. This characteristic provides the catalyst for life change in Jesus Christ. Hebrews 10:24 says, "Let us consider how we may spur one another on toward love and good deeds." "Spur" is not a soft word! It means to prod, goad or jab into action. That's not to say that we spur others in a harsh or careless way, but challenging others boldly may not always be easy or pleasant. Consider the following conversation between two men who are spiritual partners.

Dan: "Hey Tom, how are you doing?"

Tom: "Not too well. I just had a horrendous blow-up with my wife."

Dan: "I'm sorry."

Tom: (Sarcastically) "Yeah, me too. I can't believe this all started over the dumb issue of washing dishes!"

Dan: "How did you leave things with Sharon?"

Tom: "Not good. We were both yelling at each other and I stomped out of the house."

Dan: "Lynn and I are not immune from this kind of thing either. But one thing I've learned the hard way is that God wants us to take the initiative to speedily resolve issues like this in our marriage."

Tom: "I know, but she can be so unreasonable at times! I was wrong, but so was she!"

Dan: "You can't let this be about blame or who's right. Your relationship with Sharon is more important than the issue. You indicated that yourself. God wants us to love and enjoy our wives and to esteem them as dearer to us than our own self or interests."

Tom: "You're right. What would you do in my place?"

Dan: "Go home right away and ask Sharon to forgive you for arguing with her, for not treating her in a loving way and for leaving the house angrily. You must do this in genuine humility and love. Hold her and tell her you're sorry and that you love her. Then, as a demonstration of your desire to love and serve her, do the dishes joyfully. If your kids heard you argue make sure you ask their forgiveness too and let them know how much you love their mother and them.

After the dust has settled, sit down and pray together and talk about how you can resolve the dish-washing issue or others like it in the future so they don't derail you again.

Will you do these things?"

Tom: "Yes, I will. Thanks."

Dan: "Great! Hey, I'll call you this evening to find out how it went. But before you go, let's pray, okay?

Father, thank you so much for my brother, Tom. Thank you for your great love for him and Sharon. I'm excited for them and all the amazing things that you have in store for them in their marriage. Please protect their relationship and prepare Sharon's heart as Tom goes to her to make things right. Thank you for Tom's broken and humble heart. And as he asks Sharon to forgive him I pray for a sweet reconciliation. May this experience propel them forward in their relationship with you and with each other. In Jesus' name we pray, amen."

The example above is bold and focuses on a particular situation needing correction and it occurred one-on-one. Let's look at the following situation and watch how Tom takes this experience a step farther and leverages it in partnership with the men in his small group. Tom leads a small group of men that meets in his home weekly. (Yes, this kind of marital discord can happen with small group leaders!) The incident above happened just a couple days before their small group met. On the night of their small group, they studied Ephesians 5:25-33.

Following the study, Tom bares his soul and confesses to the men in his small group how he had acted earlier that week in an unloving way toward his wife and about the argument that followed. He then tells them how he talked to Dan and what Dan told him to do. Tom shares that he followed through with Dan's challenge and the result was that he and Sharon were reconciled that night.

Tom tells them further how he experienced great joy from the Lord when he humbled himself and loved Sharon sacrificially. Tom finishes his story by challenging the men in his small group, "Guys, what the Scripture says here in Ephesians 5 is real and relevant and it works! We have got to love our wives sacrificially every day, putting aside our own needs if necessary. Are you with me?"

What Tom did with his small group is very powerful! He demonstrated authentic living before these men and confessed his own shortcomings. He then testified boldly how God worked in his marriage and finally challenged his men to follow his example. He also demonstrated his willingness to yield to God's leading through a bold challenge by his brother, Dan. This model of challenging others boldly in God's truth leverages God's power to change lives. By doing this, Tom drew these men into spiritual partnership with him and boldly challenged them to follow Christ in loving their wives.

Because spiritual partnerships are not hierarchical but mutual and reciprocal, spiritual partners recognize that they both are needy before the Lord. This sense of neediness humbles us and puts us in a frame of mind to receive a bold challenge from each other. In fact, we hunger for it!

Boldly challenging our spiritual partners is not always so directive, however. Sometimes a bold challenge may take the form of a suggestion like, "What if you were to go home and ask Sharon to forgive you regardless of whether she owns up to her role in the argument?" At other times, we may challenge each other boldly with a question like, "What do you think God would have you do in this situation?" We can also challenge each other to "follow me, as I follow Christ." This is a biblical pattern that's very powerful. This is how the Word of God is spoken and demonstrated through our lives for others to see and mimic.

In our spiritual partnerships, we rely heavily on the Holy Spirit to speak to us and lead us in our conversations with each other. Follow his lead.

In the next chapter we'll consider what spiritual partnerships look like.

Discussion Questions

1. What particular point in this chapter impacted you most?

2. If you are working through this book with others, have two of you role-play the conversation found at the beginning of this chapter. How did Dan boldly challenge Tom in this situation? How effective was it?

3. In this chapter, the story continues to unfold with Tom. In what way did Tom boldly challenge his small group from God's Word? How effective was it?

4. Rob has mentioned several times that spiritual partnerships are *mutual* and *reciprocal* rather than hierarchical. What does this mean and why is it so important to build our spiritual partnerships in this way?

5. Think of an area in your life in which you need to be boldly challenged from God's Word. Share this with someone and ask them to challenge you boldly from God's Word.

Chapter Five
WHAT DOES SPIRITUAL PARTNERSHIP LOOK LIKE?

As iron sharpens iron, so one person sharpens another.
– Proverbs 27:17 –

After cultivating numerous spiritual partnerships over a period of eleven years, I still find it awkward to develop a relationship with a new spiritual partner! And I know that I'm not alone in this. There are a number of reasons for this sense of awkwardness. One is that we rarely seem to pursue a relationship with someone intentionally. We often just let relationships happen serendipitously.

Another reason for this awkward feeling is that spiritual partners both know that they are stepping into a relationship in which high levels of mutual vulnerability and trust must reign. Merely left to themselves, relationships will rarely reach that level of familiarity and impact. Beginning a spiritual partnership at the transformational relationship level feels different—even scary at first!

Another reason that spiritual partnerships may seem awkward initially is that we don't know how to proceed. A spiritual partnership may feel contrived or stiff in the beginning. In fact, I can almost guarantee that your initial meetings with your spiritual partner will feel awkward! So when you sense those feelings, just remember I told you it would be like that and press on. Soon you'll forget you ever had such feelings.

Getting through that awkward stage and growing your relationship requires hard and deliberate work. Let me share with you what we did and what I've found to work well over the past eleven years. Keep in mind that you can either upgrade a current relationship to a spiritual partnership, or initiate a new relationship to launch your spiritual partnership. Either way, you must be *deliberate* about it.

Begin by being very clear about why you're partnering together. Verbalize with each other why you are establishing this relationship. *The purpose of your spiritual partnership is to propel each other into deeper relationship with Christ.* You want to "sharpen" each other (Proverbs 27:17) and "spur" each other in becoming more Christlike (Hebrews 10:24).

With the above in mind, agree to always be open and honest with each other. Openly express your mutual confidentiality. Be transparent with each other and trust each other in confidence that what you share will not go any further. Leave no area of your life untouched or hidden from each other. This is vital to your spiritual growth and is at the core of why we need spiritual partners. "Therefore confess your sins to each other and pray for each other so that you may be healed. The prayer of a righteous person is powerful and effective." (James 5:16)

In your initial meetings, just get to know each other. Share your life stories and practice good listening skills. Find out how your spiritual partner came to Christ; what his/her childhood was like. Ask about their career; relationships, etc. From the start always pray for each other. If your spiritual partner shares an immediate need, stop and pray for him/her on the spot. In this way too, prayer becomes an on-going conversation rather than a "thing we do at the end."

As you continue to meet, be sure to spend time together in real life. Give each other permission to speak into one another's lives and to ask tough questions. By *tough questions*, I mean questions like:

- ▶ If you could pinpoint anything in your life right now that is stealing your joy in Christ what would it be?
- ▶ What is God doing in your life right now?
- ▶ What has God been revealing to you about himself from his Word?
- ▶ What habit, thought pattern, or sin in your life is "eating your lunch?"
- ▶ How's your relationship with your spouse?
- ▶ What can I pray with you about?
- ▶ To what extent are you representing Christ well at work?

Let's take a closer look at these questions for a moment. Notice first that all of these questions and those that I listed earlier in this book are *open-ended questions*. Open-ended questions cannot be answered with "yes," or "no," but require explanation. Yes-or-no questions are called *closed-ended questions*, because they *close* the discussion rather than opening it. We want to open up discussion and keep it open.

Also, consider the difference between the following two questions: 1) "Have you been reading God's Word lately?" This is a closed-ended question, answerable by "yes," or "no," so it stifles on-going conversation. But did you notice also that this question has a twinge of judgment or guilt attached to it?

Contrast the previous question with this one: 2) "What has God been showing you from his Word lately?" This is an open-ended question. Even if the person has not been in the Word, it invites honesty. But this question does something much more. The first question refers to a *task*, "Have you been reading God's Word lately." The second question speaks of *relationship*, "What has God been showing you from his Word lately?" The first question may make a person *feel guilty* about not reading the Bible, but the second question makes one *yearn* to hear from God. I hope the contrast between those two questions demonstrates how important our questions are and how they can also *instruct* us.

Also, let's say that I'm out hiking with one of my spiritual partners and I ask him, "What's God been doing in your life?" Because spiritual partnerships are mutual and reciprocal, I don't ask that question just to *check up on him*. I genuinely want to know about his relationship with the Lord and how he has been interacting with God. I'll also expect him to ask me the same or a similar question. If I get lengthy silence after that question, I may say something like, "While you're thinking of a response, let me share with you what God has been doing in my life." That takes the immediate pressure off and models for my spiritual partner the mutual and reciprocal nature of our partnership. After I share I may come back and ask, "So how about you? What's God been doing in your life?"

In the previous example, notice that it's okay to take the lead in the conversation even though our spiritual partnership is mutual and reciprocal. The fact is one of you will always have to take the lead for anything to happen. Share that leadership with your spiritual partner so that either of you can initiate the conversation.

Let's also consider follow-up questions for a moment. If in response to my question, "What's God been doing in your life lately?" my spiritual partner says something like, "I don't know. God seems distant lately." What I'll do is come back with another open-ended question: "What do you attribute that to?" Or, "Why do you think that is?" Or, "When was the last time you felt close to God?" In all our conversations with our spiritual partners we want to rely on the Holy Spirit to lead us. We also want to express genuine love and empathy with our spiritual partner. In such a case it's always appropriate to pray for your spiritual partner in a sincere, life-giving way.

Let's look at another approach to a response like, "I don't know. God seems distant lately." If I have ever felt like that (who hasn't?), now might be a great time to be transparent about it with my spiritual partner. I'll tell him how I felt and how God led me out of my funk. What I want to communicate here is that we're never condescending or arrogant. Spiritual partnership is a *mutual* and *reciprocal* relationship in which we both rely on the Holy Spirit to help us spur one another into deeper relationship with Christ.

Please don't let the above examples scare you off if you don't consider yourself skilled in the formation of open-ended questions! All we're talking about here is conducting a purposeful conversation. Let the Holy Spirit teach you and lead you. And learn from each other.

When you ask open-ended questions like those above, you may be shocked sometimes with what your spiritual partner shares—but don't act shocked! Stand by him and pray with him. Always pray for each other! Keep 1 Corinthians 10:12 in mind, "Therefore let anyone who thinks that he stands take heed lest he fall." (ESV)

Also, consider Galatians 6:1-2 NLT:

> *Dear brothers and sisters, if another believer is overcome by some sin, you who are godly should gently and humbly help that person back onto the right path. And be careful not to fall into the same temptation yourself. Share each other's burdens, and in this way obey the law of Christ.*

Keep up with each other on what is going on in your various relationships and aspects of life. Always, praying with and for each other. Expect God to work in powerful ways in your lives and celebrate it when he does.

Over the years I've enjoyed multiple spiritual partnerships with men in Alaska and Washington State. Without breaching confidentiality, let me share with you what some of my spiritual partnerships have looked like. I've already told you about Ed and our Friday afternoon hikes. Perry is another man I partnered with in Alaska, and then again in Washington when he moved here. We meet weekly in a coffee house at 6:30am. We discuss our struggles and victories, challenge one another, and pray for each other. Perry and I have also had the privilege of working on a couple of book projects together. My wife and I enjoy getting together with Perry and Susan (his wife) whenever we can.

Greg was one of my primary hiking buddies in Alaska and he mentored me in extreme winter alpine hiking. Greg and I almost always met together in the context of a hike, but our conversations were rich and full. Greg is a year or two older than I am. Greg and I especially enjoyed discussing Scripture and how God was speaking to us through his Word. As we prayed together, we watched God transform individuals that either Greg or I were working with. When Greg got married, I had the privilege of performing his wedding.

Ron was another pastor in town and perhaps ten years my senior. We met weekly in my office for nearly four years. The time I spent with Ron was very rich, refreshing, and I always felt like I had the most to gain from our spiritual partnership, but I know he'd tell you otherwise. We talked "shop", discussed Scripture, shared our common challenges and prayed for each other. God used Ron numerous times to speak truth into my life. Ron is now retired and lives in Massachusetts, but we still stay in contact and I highly value his friendship.

Jay and I spent time as spiritual partners in a wide variety of settings including hiking, coffee shops, in my office and his. Jay is a strong leader and very influential in the lives of many men and women. He is perhaps 15 years younger than I am. I've also gone backpacking and fishing with Jay. We've both grown a lot in each other's company. When we lived in Alaska, we enjoyed sharing a meal together as couples as often as we could.

Dave is the first man with whom I partnered spiritually when I moved back to Spokane. I had known him in Alaska as well, but we deepened our relationship in Washington. For over five years, our routine has been to meet every Thursday morning at 6am to walk our neighborhood and pray. We share what's going on in our lives and courageously challenge each other. My wife and I are close friends with Dave and Muna (his wife). We often share meals, go boating, camping, and vacation together. For the past few months, Dave's job has required him to be out of town weekly, so our meetings are on hold until his schedule changes. We both look forward to meeting each week again. In the mean time we text and pray for each other.

When I first met Ray, the Lord was drawing Ray back to himself. It was a joy to watch the Lord then use Ray to woo his wife back into deep relationship with the Lord.

We began meeting as spiritual partners nearly six years ago. We usually meet in my office or a coffee shop. We always prompt each other with a great question like, "What has God been doing in your life?" And then we share those stories with each other. We hold each other up in prayer and have watched the Lord do some amazing things in our lives and the lives of those within our spheres of influence.

Chris, Jeff, Paul B., and Paul C. are other men with whom I've partnered spiritually over the years. With some of them, we met around a Bible study or a read through the Bible. In every case I've personally benefited in a huge way from hanging out with these guys in the presence of Jesus. We've challenged each other, demonstrated tangibly our Christlike love toward each other and our families. I'm deeply indebted to all these men for the way they've spurred me on in my walk with Christ. I know I'm a better man today in Christ, because of these men.

Above, I've told you about my spiritual partners over the past eleven years. I want to communicate how natural, enjoyable and meaningful these partnerships have been. Please notice too that each partnership has been different. We've met at a wide variety of times and places and often with different agendas. Yet, all spiritual partnerships have one thing in common: *we always seek to propel each other into deeper relationship with Jesus Christ*.

By the way, there's another benefit of spiritual partnerships that I haven't mentioned yet. In every one of the above spiritual partnerships the wives of these men are delighted that their husbands are spiritually partnered with another man who is pursuing Christ! Spiritual partnerships lead to strong marriages and healthy relationships all the way around because they center on becoming more like Christ.

Men, we also need to gently encourage our wives to cultivate spiritual partnerships with other women who are following Christ. Notice I said, "*gently* encourage our wives!" If we are leading by example and they see what Christ is doing in us through our spiritual partner, our wives will hunger for similar transformational relationships. We can also make it easier for our wives to cultivate a spiritual partnership by watching the kids, doing their chores, and generally freeing them up.

On the following pages are some frequently asked questions about spiritual partnership and then four simple steps for helping you launch a spiritual partnership.

Discussion Questions

1. What particular point in this chapter impacted you most?

2. What are some reasons we might find it awkward when initiating a spiritual partnership?

3. What advice does Rob give about how to launch a spiritual partnership?

4. Explain the difference between open- and closed-ended questions. What happens when we pose open-ended questions (like those listed) with our spiritual partner?

5. Rob shared some examples of spiritual partnerships he has enjoyed over the years. What are some key characteristics of spiritual partnerships that you glean from his examples?

6. Rob mentions another benefit of spiritual partnerships in terms of improved marriages. Why do you suppose that spiritual partnerships have this positive effect on marriages?

FAQ's about Partnerships

Q: How often should we meet?

A: I recommend once a week, but be flexible as need be.

Q: Why do we insist on gender-specific partnerships?

A: We have found through much experience that people find it easier to be vulnerable and relate better with those of the same gender. Also, many issues would be inappropriate and make us vulnerable to temptation if we shared them with someone of the opposite sex. Gender-specific partnerships were Jesus' pattern.

Q: How long should/could a partnership exist?

A: Some partnerships are established for a specific period of time (e.g., three months, six months, one year, etc.), while others might last years. You may want to start with a specific time period in mind and expand from there.

Q: What are some ideas on where to meet with my partner?

A: Meet wherever works best for you – at home, go somewhere, or do something together, a restaurant, coffee shop, a park, etc. Avoid places or activities that are distracting.

Q: How do I find a spiritual partner?

A: Start by praying and asking God for a spiritual partnership. If no one comes to mind, start asking around in your church. Ask your pastor for ideas. Consider "upgrading" a current relationship you have with someone. When you find a guy with whom you would like to partner, ask him, "I am looking for someone to partner with me so I can grow in Christ. Would you be willing to partner spiritually with me?"

Q: What do we do when we meet together?

A: The goal of the partnership is to propel each other toward a deeper relationship with Christ. There are numerous activities that can help you achieve this. (E.g., commit to reading through the New Testament or whole Bible together over a period of time; read a book together and discuss it; go on a hike, drive, or walk with each other and share and pray as you go; pray with each other; help each other with projects around the house; get your spouses/families together for a meal; etc.) The sky is the limit. Be creative, flexible, use variety and stay on track!

Q: Do men have an easier time partnering spiritually than women do or vice-versa?

A: In my experience talking with hundreds of men and women about spiritual partnerships, neither men nor women find it any easier or more difficult. The concept of spiritual partnership has been foreign to many of us in the past, so partnering spiritually may seem awkward initially to *anyone*. But soon, you will wonder why you waited so long! Also, do not fall into the trap of using a reserved personality as an excuse for not partnering.

Q: What's the difference between partnering and mentoring?

A: A mentoring relationship assumes that one who is more experienced mentors or disciples another who is not as experienced. A partnering relationship assumes that those in the relationship are peers in their walk with the Lord. Spiritual partnership is mutual and reciprocal.

LAUNCH YOUR SPIRITUAL PARTNERSHIP

The intent of this chapter is to simply get you launched into a spiritual partnership. You can either follow the steps below in sequence, or skip those that you've already tackled and move on to the next step. I pray that you discover quickly the rich benefits from spiritual partnership for both you and the person you partner with spiritually.

Step One: If you don't have a spiritual partner, tell the Lord that you recognize your need for spiritual partnership and ask him to direct you to the individual with whom you should partner spiritually. The Lord wants us in transformational relationships like this, so this isn't a prayer to determine *whether to partner spiritually!* Because of this, look around you. Who makes the most sense for you to partner with? You might choose to upgrade a current relationship to spiritual partnership, or you may ask someone whom you don't yet know well. Remember, men partner spiritually with men, and women with women.

Step Two: Approach someone and ask them to partner with you spiritually. If your potential spiritual partner isn't familiar with spiritual partnerships, go through this book together as a great way to launch your spiritual partnership. Be very clear about why you're partnering together. Verbalize with each other why you are establishing this relationship. The purpose of your spiritual partnership is to propel each other into deeper relationship with Christ. You want to "sharpen" each other (Proverbs 27:17) and "spur" each other in becoming more Christlike (Hebrews 10:24).

Step Three: Decide when, where, and how often you'll meet and agree on a general pattern of your meetings together. I recommend that you meet weekly. Set a time that works well for both of you and make it a priority to be there. If you're married, explain to your spouse why you're meeting with this person. Don't over-plan your times together. Instead, come up with a basic pattern and be flexible to change it as you need to.

Step Four: Start meeting regularly. Spur each other on to Christlikeness. Enter into this relationship with a sense of expectation that God will do powerful things to root out sin, transform ungodly patterns, and make you both more like Jesus! Ensure that you weave the five characteristics of spiritual partnerships into your relationship:

- ▶ Men with men and women with women pursuing relationship with Christ
- ▶ Spend time together in real life
- ▶ Love and care for each other
- ▶ Challenge each other boldly from God's Word
- ▶ Pray with and for each other

Remember, people are most likely to change in the context of *transformational relationships*. So, move to transformational relationship the first time you meet by giving each other permission to ask tough questions like:

- "What is God doing in your life right now?"
- "What is God showing you from his Word?"
- "What one thing in your life is preventing you from enjoying God fully?"
- "In what ways are you currently leading your wife and family closer to the Lord?"
- "How well are you loving your wife right now?"
- "What are your greatest joys/challenges in walking with Jesus right now?"
- "What's one thing you'd like to see Christ change in you?"
- "In what ways is God using you to model Christlikeness to others?"

As you pray for each other, experiment with and adhere to the characteristics of conversational prayer with each other. Those characteristics are:

- Pray short, phrase or sentence prayers.
- Stay on a theme until it seems right to move on. Piggyback on each other's prayers.
- Keep your prayers vertical (don't use prayer to *preach* at others).

- Embrace silence as an opportunity to listen to God, transition, or process what's been prayed. Listen to the Holy Spirit and each other.

- Believe the best of each other.

I'm excited for you as you step into or continue a transformational relationship with your spiritual partner. Expect God to work powerfully in your spiritual partnership. Be sure to let others know what God is doing in your lives as a result of your spiritual partnership.

If this book has helped you in your walk with Christ, please pass it along to others. If you'd like to tell me about what Christ is doing in your spiritual partnership, please contact me at ***www.fischerlifecoaching.com.***

And let us consider how we may spur one another on toward love and good deeds, not giving up meeting together, as some are in the habit of doing, but encouraging one another—and all the more as you see the Day approaching.
— Hebrews 10:24-25 —

81

OTHER BOOKS BY ROB FISCHER

Rogue Principles that Grow Church Community – A small group curriculum and companion book to the movie *Rogue Saints*

Enthralled with God, 2nd Edition with Discussion Questions

Strategies for Discipleship – A Small Group Curriculum that Targets the Skills for Discipling Others

Becoming Tarzan – A humorous collection of childhood stories that appeal to the whole family

13 Jars – The true stories of women who found redemption, forgiveness and peace through Jesus Christ following their abortions

To contact Rob visit him online at:
www.fischerlifecoaching.com.

Made in the USA
Columbia, SC
22 August 2018